The Great Pause

Perseverance Through the Pandemic

Julia Manini, Ed.D & Anne-Joyelle Occhicone

Illustrator: Laura Catrinella

MW01519250

One Printers Way
Altona, MB R0G 0B0
Canada

www.friesenpress.com

Copyright © 2022 by Julia Manini and Anne-Joyelle Occhicone
First Edition — 2022

All rights reserved.

No part of this publication may be reproduced in any form, or by any means, electronic or mechanical, including photocopying, recording, or any information browsing, storage, or retrieval system, without permission in writing from FriesenPress.

ISBN
978-1-03-911725-9 (Hardcover)
978-1-03-911724-2 (Paperback)
978-1-03-911726-6 (eBook)

1. JUVENILE NONFICTION, PHILOSOPHY

Distributed to the trade by The Ingram Book Company

In honour of all that was found and lost.

For Tullio, Vienna, and Serafina...all that I actually needed.

-AJO

For my beloved boys, Mario, Teodoro, and Elisio...who continue to teach me that life happens side, by side, by side.

-JM(P2)

_____

_____

_____

_____

The whole world was busy being busy, too busy. And so, they did not notice; they did not breathe deeply, and they did not pause.

Until something happened to one person, then to another, and then to the whole world. And it was as though everything just stood still.

The swings that once seemed as though they swung straight up to the sun slowed to a gentle sway.

Grass once trodden and flattened by gleeful feet stood upright, each blade blanketing the earth without bend.

Streets once alive with the steady flow of people emptied to spaces where the lines between each sidewalk slab could be counted as far as the eye could see.

Bakeries that once stirred the skies with smells of freshly made sweetness now closed to leave an unperfumed air of quiet.

Classrooms once bustling with the energy of curious minds grew tired and dull in their emptiness.

And those large gatherings of smiles, handshakes, hugs, and kisses seemed to altogether disappear into the distances created by the great pause.

It seemed as though the whole world held its breath as bright minds shaped lives into foreign patterns that called for a different way of being.

Footsteps of fear crept in as people inched toward these new and unfamiliar ways.

Tears filled the oceans as sad hearts said farewell from afar and the air became heavy as hands waved their final goodbyes.

But day by day, the heaviness gave way to the light of humanity that glimmered in each space created by the great pause.

The glimmers became beacons of light as people rose to the challenge in ways that shaped the patterns and waves into curves of hope.

Heroes revealed themselves in grocery stores, hospitals, factories, and buses. While most did their part and stayed in, the heroes stepped out to bravely take on what mattered most.

Leaders once separated by water, fences, or ideas united to champion a common purpose that focused on the sameness among us.

Purpose inspired innovators to see creative solutions where, at first glance, only challenges could be found.

Care and compassion filled the distance between loved ones and strangers alike. Balconies became bridges, connecting neighbours through song and good cheer.

Time wrapped around parents and their children, filling scheduled and routine spaces with moments nestled in togetherness and wonder.

Patience and ingenuity guided learning and working into reimagined spaces beyond buildings and walls.

And trees and flowers, once weighed down by the world's frenzied busyness, smiled in the stillness, breathing in the crisp, nourishing air.

So while the great pause was but a moment in time its impact could be felt for a lifetime. For in the loss of so much of what was known, much was found.

In the loss of distraction, people found quiet moments to notice.

In the loss of busyness people found beauty in simplicity.

In the loss of what had been taken for granted people found appreciation.

In the loss of boundaries people found each other.

And so they began to breathe out slowly, changed forever by a moment shared by the whole world.

A moment that called for each person to rise up to all that had been found and lost when everything else became quiet.

The reminder of the great pause echoed in the minds and hearts of all, and there was not a space or a moment that was ever the same again.

The End

"The Great Pause is a book that belongs in everyone's home. It is a gentle reminder that nothing is more powerful than the human spirit. It is a great teaching tool for young people to understand that obstacles and challenges are an invitation for deeper connection, understanding and kindness."
– Theo Koffler, author of The RETHiNK Kit
and founder of Mindfulness Without Borders

About the Authors

Anne-Joyelle Occhicone and Julia Manini are, respectively, a developer of social policy and a doctor of educational leadership. The authors endeavour to practice a way of being that offers growth and a hopeful perspective to those they encounter. They are seekers of wisdom, honouring those who set out as change-makers. Most importantly, they are mothers raising another generation of spirited individuals to honour the complexity of the human condition.

The pandemic offered a platform for innovation, reflection, and connection, inspiring this written work. With The Great Pause, the authors seek to explore our shared experience during a time of immense challenge.

Julia Manini and Anne-Joyelle Occhicone both live in Toronto, Canada, with their husbands and children, surrounded by the support and love of family and friends.

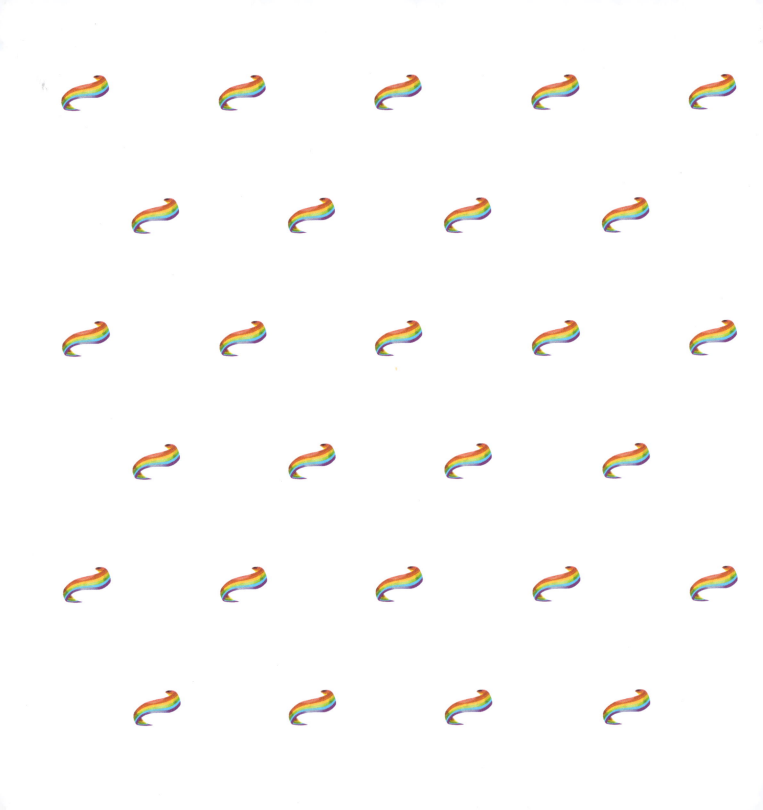

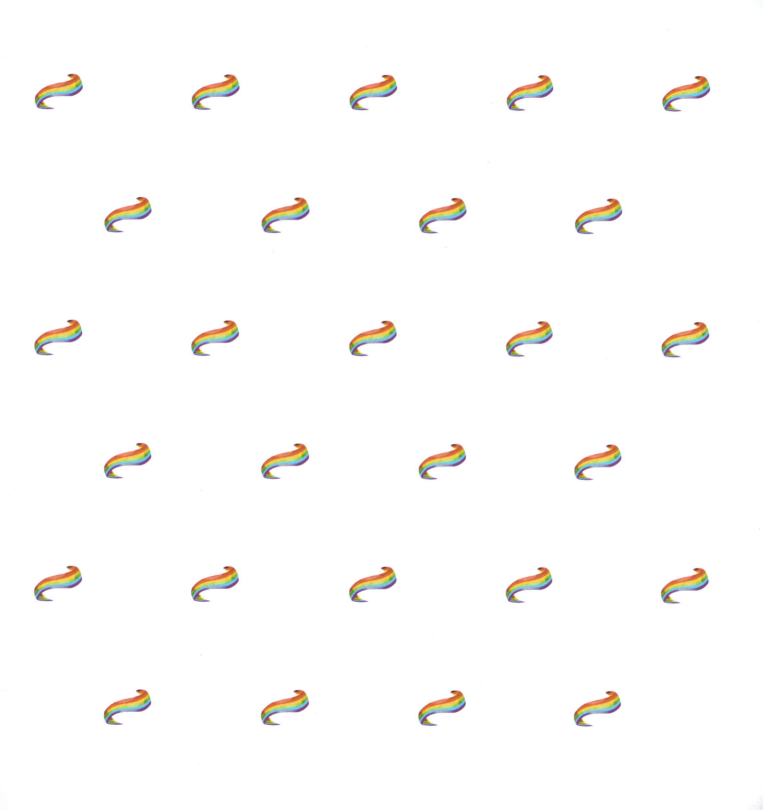

CPSIA information can be obtained
at www.ICGtesting.com
Printed in the USA
LVHW070255270922
729371LV00002B/34

9 781039 117242